I0606111

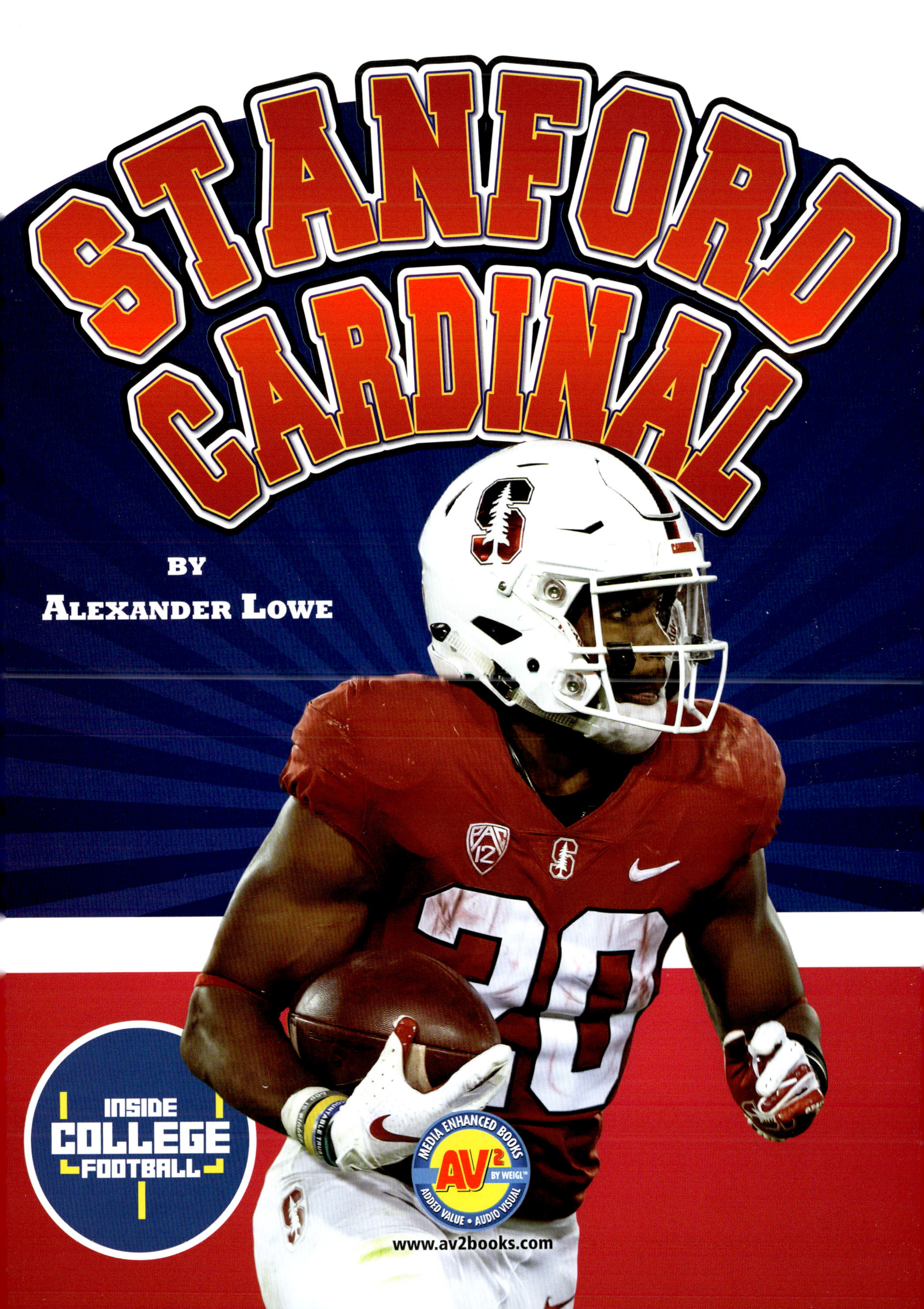
STANFORD
CARDINAL
BY
ALEXANDER LOWE
INSIDE
COLLEGE
FOOTBALL
MEDIA ENHANCED BOOKS
AV2
BY WEIGL
ADDED VALUE • AUDIO VISUAL
www.av2books.com

Go to **www.av2books.com,** and enter this book's unique code.

BOOK CODE

AVL77889

AV² by Weigl brings you media enhanced books that support active learning.

AV² provides enriched content that supplements and complements this book. Weigl's AV² books strive to create inspired learning and engage young minds in a total learning experience.

Your AV² Media Enhanced books come alive with...

Audio
Listen to sections of the book read aloud.

Key Words
Study vocabulary, and complete a matching word activity.

Video
Watch informative video clips.

Quizzes
Test your knowledge.

Embedded Weblinks
Gain additional information for research.

Slideshow
View images and captions, and prepare a presentation.

Try This!
Complete activities and hands-on experiments.

... and much, much more!

Published by AV² by Weigl
350 5th Avenue, 59th Floor
New York, NY 10118
Website: www.av2books.com

Library of Congress Control Number: 2018968212

ISBN 978-1-7911-0099-5 (hardcover)
ISBN 978-1-7911-0100-8 (multi-user eBook)
ISBN 978-1-7911-0101-5 (single-user eBook)

Printed in Guangzhou, China
1 2 3 4 5 6 7 8 9 0 23 22 21 20 19

042019
102318

Project Coordinator: Jared Siemens   Designer: Terry Paulhus

Every reasonable effort has been made to trace ownership and to obtain permission to reprint copyright material. The publishers would be pleased to have any errors or omissions brought to their attention so that they may be corrected in subsequent printings.

The publisher acknowledges Alamy, Getty Images, and Wikimedia Commons as its primary image suppliers for this title.

Stanford Cardinal

CONTENTS

Introduction

Football has been a part of Stanford University since the first team took the field in 1891. Since then, the team has won 746 games and 15 bowl games. It has also produced many players who have gone on to play in the National Football League (NFL).

The team plays its games in Stanford, California, against the tough competition of the Pacific-12 (Pac-12) Conference. Stanford University is consistently ranked in the top 10 academically across the nation. Its students are some of the brightest in the nation.

While many schools have nicknames or mascots that are animals, Stanford is simply the Cardinal. Cardinal is a deep shade of red. Since it is hard to dress up as a color, the school's marching band thought a tree would be a good representative of the area and school. Ever since its first appearance in 1975, a student in a tree costume has been on the field, leading the band in cheering on the team.

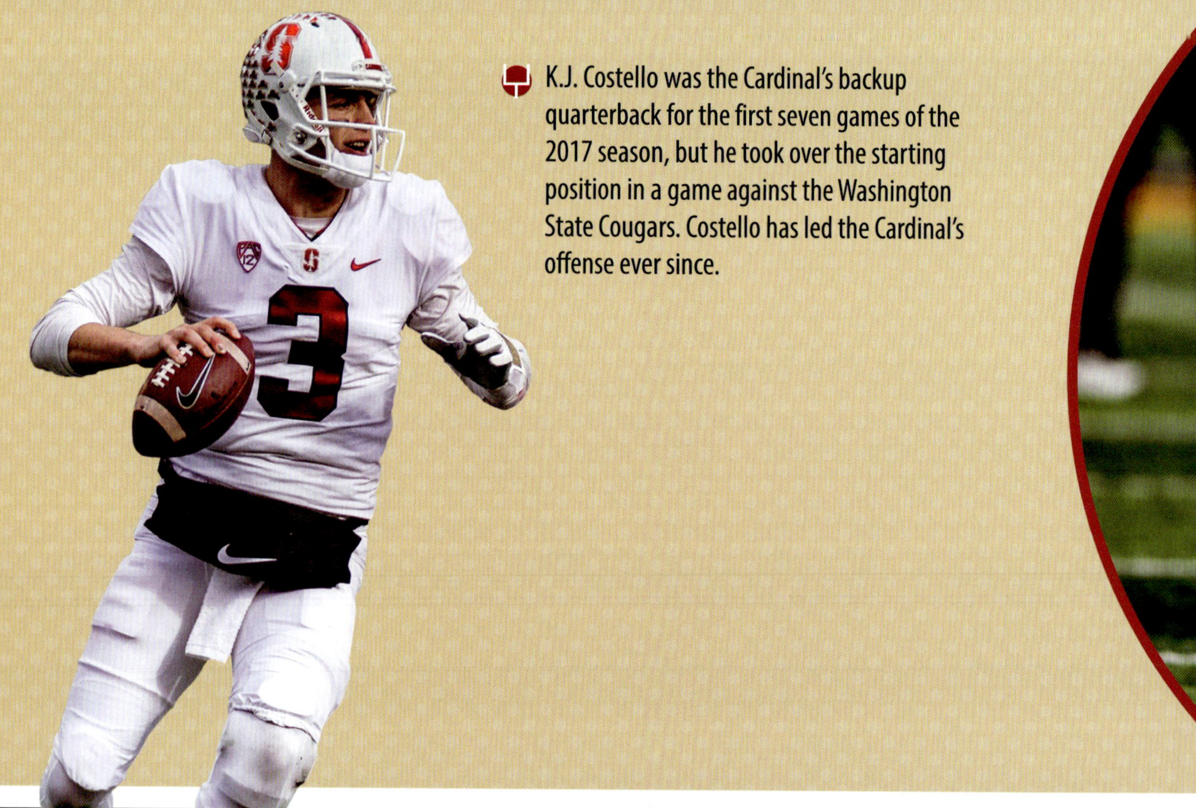

K.J. Costello was the Cardinal's backup quarterback for the first seven games of the 2017 season, but he took over the starting position in a game against the Washington State Cougars. Costello has led the Cardinal's offense ever since.

Cornerback Paulson Adebo played in 13 games and logged 64 tackles during Stanford's 2018 season.

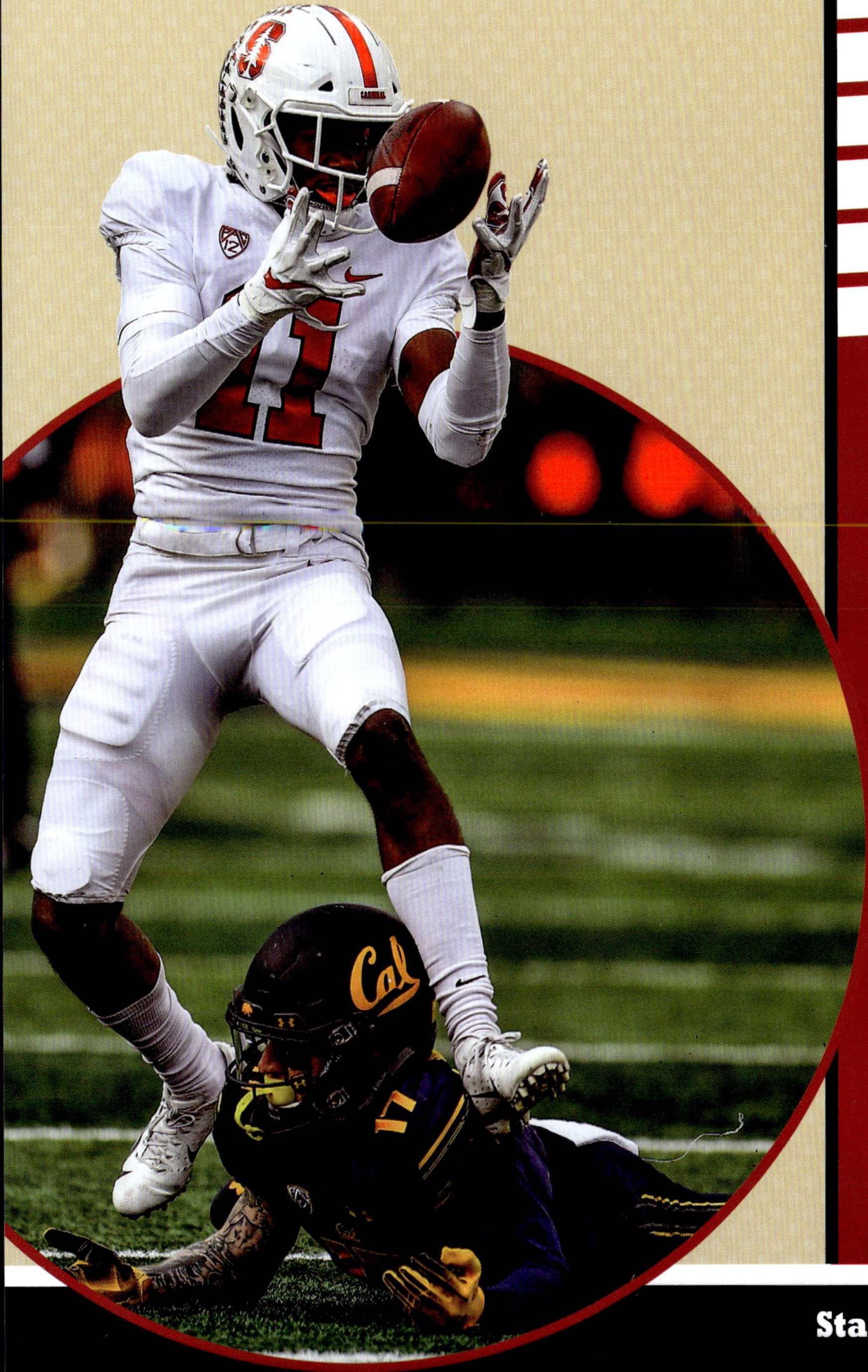

STANFORD

Stadium Stanford Stadium

Division Pacific-12 (Pac-12) North

Head Coach David Shaw

Location Stanford, California

National Championships 0

Nicknames Stanford, the Cardinal

25
First-Round NFL Draft Picks

1
Heisman Memorial Trophy Winner

30
Bowl Game Appearances

30
NFL Draft Picks Since 2018

History

Stanford won two-straight **Rose Bowls** in 1970 and 1971, beating the University of Michigan Wolverines and Ohio State University Buckeyes.

Stanford has had many prominent coaches throughout the team's history, including Glenn Scobey "Pop" Warner. He held the record for most wins in the National Collegiate Athletic Association (NCAA) for decades, and gave his name to the most popular youth football program in the United States.

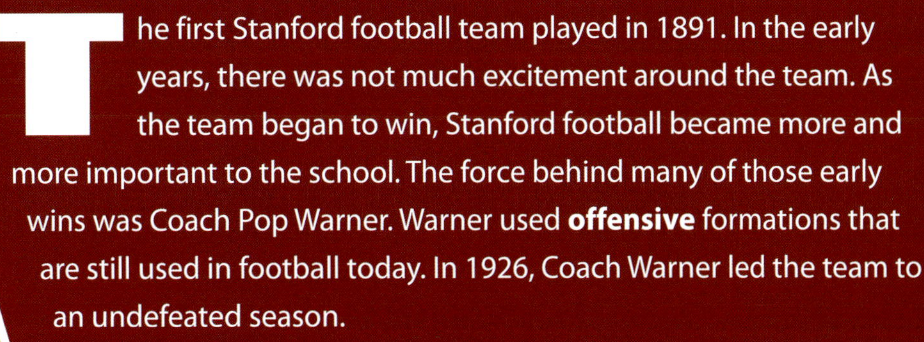

The first Stanford football team played in 1891. In the early years, there was not much excitement around the team. As the team began to win, Stanford football became more and more important to the school. The force behind many of those early wins was Coach Pop Warner. Warner used **offensive** formations that are still used in football today. In 1926, Coach Warner led the team to an undefeated season.

From the 1920s through 1940, the Cardinal were a staple of the Rose Bowl, reaching that game seven times. The 1950s and 1960s were not as successful for Stanford, but Coach John Ralston got the team back into bowl games in the 1970s. It has been one of the nation's best college football programs ever since.

In 2011, David Shaw was named the head coach. The team won three consecutive bowl games over the next few years. At the end of the 2015 season, the Cardinal were ranked third in the nation. That was its highest final ranking in 75 years. Coach Shaw now has the Stanford record for most wins and continues adding to that total every year.

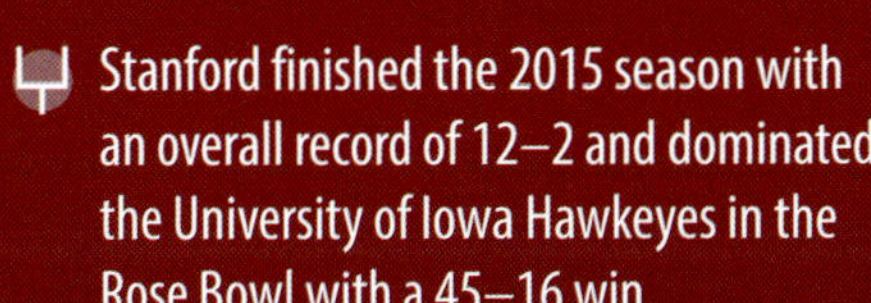

Stanford finished the 2015 season with an overall record of 12–2 and dominated the University of Iowa Hawkeyes in the Rose Bowl with a 45–16 win.

The Stadium

Construction of the new Stanford Stadium began minutes after the Cardinal's last game of the 2005 season, and was finished in time for their second game of the 2006 season, just 10 months later.

Stanford Stadium has been the home of the Cardinal since it opened in the 1921 season. The initial version of the stadium cost around $500,000. It could seat 60,000 fans in a horseshoe shape. Later, multiple expansions and **renovations** took place, including closing the horseshoe into a full bowl in 1925. Scoreboards were added in 1978.

The mild weather of Stanford makes Stanford Stadium a great place to play and watch football. In addition to Stanford football games, the stadium hosted some events during the 1984 Summer Olympics, the 1985 Super Bowl, and multiple soccer **World Cup** games over the decades.

In 2005, Stanford Stadium was rebuilt, bringing fans closer to the action than ever before. The old stadium had a track around the football field that was removed during the renovation. The stadium opened in time for the 2006 Cardinal season. The $90-million stadium has more than 50,000 seats for fans to cheer on their team. In 2013, high definition (HD) video scoreboards were added, bringing modern technology to the fan experience.

In its early days, Stanford Stadium seated more than 85,000 fans. In 1935, about 94,000 people filled the stadium to watch Stanford defeat the University of California.

Where They Play

Welcome to Stanford Stadium, home of the Cardinal. Students and fans dressed in red fill the stands on game days. Stanford's marching band blasts rock-and-roll tunes as the team takes to the field. The Tree dances on the sideline as the game begins. Unique traditions and a passion for winning bring fans together each season to cheer for the Cardinal at Stanford Stadium.

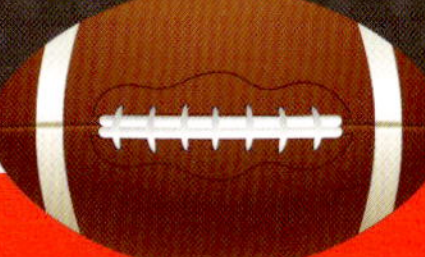

PAC-12 NORTH

1. **Oregon State University**
   Corvallis, Oregon
2. ★ **Stanford University**
   Stanford, California
3. **University of California**
   Berkeley, California
4. **University of Oregon**
   Eugene, Oregon
5. **University of Washington**
   Seattle, Washington
6. **Washington State University**
   Pullman, Washington

Arena
Stanford Stadium

Location
Stanford, California

Broke Ground
June, 1921

Completed
November, 1921

Surface
Real Grass

Features
- 50,424 seating capacity
- Student section called the "Red Zone"
- 1,673-foot (510-meter) ribbon board that shows scores and stats

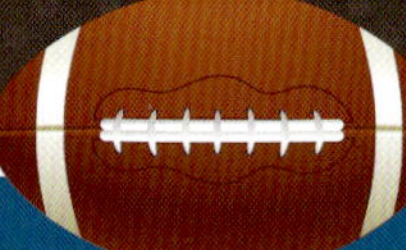

PAC-12 SOUTH

1. **Arizona State University**
   Tempe, Arizona
2. **University of Arizona**
   Tucson, Arizona
3. **University of California, Los Angeles**
   Los Angeles, California
4. **University of Colorado Boulder**
   Boulder, Colorado
5. **University of Southern California**
   Los Angeles, California
6. **University of Utah**
   Salt Lake City, Utah

WASHINGTON
OREGON
IDAHO
MONTANA
NORTH DAKOTA
SOUTH DAKOTA
MINNESOTA
WISCONSIN
WYOMING
NEVADA
UTAH
COLORADO
NEBRASKA
IOWA
KANSAS
MISSOURI
CALIFORNIA
ARIZONA
NEW MEXICO
OKLAHOMA
ARKANSAS
TEXAS
LOUISIANA
Pacific Ocean
LEGEND
Home Stadium
Pac-12 North
Pac-12 South
United States
Other Countries
Water
SCALE
0 miles
500 miles
0 kilometers
500 km

The Uniforms

Football helmets did not have **ear holes** until 1915. They were added to allow players to hear each other.

The Cardinal first wore one of Nike's "pro-combat" all-black uniforms during their 2010 season. Although players and fans prefer the traditional cardinal and white, Stanford takes the field in an all-black uniform in one game each season, usually against a tough rival.

Stanford's Cardinal nickname relates to the color of its uniforms. Stanford usually wears a cardinal jersey with white pants for home games and a white jersey with white pants for away games. Their helmets are white with a cardinal red stripe down the middle, and the team **logo** is on both sides. The Stanford team logo is a block "S" with a tree in the center.

AWAY

The Cardinal have not made many changes to what the team wears over the years. Instead, its classic look has remained consistent. The uniforms have always been some combination of white and cardinal. The most recent change to the classic uniforms was a black outline around the jersey numbers. In 2010, the team also introduced an all-black alternate uniform.

The Cardinal's helmets sometimes include stickers called Stanford Axes. Those stickers are given to players who do something outstanding in a game. Getting a helmet full of axe stickers can be a great honor for a player.

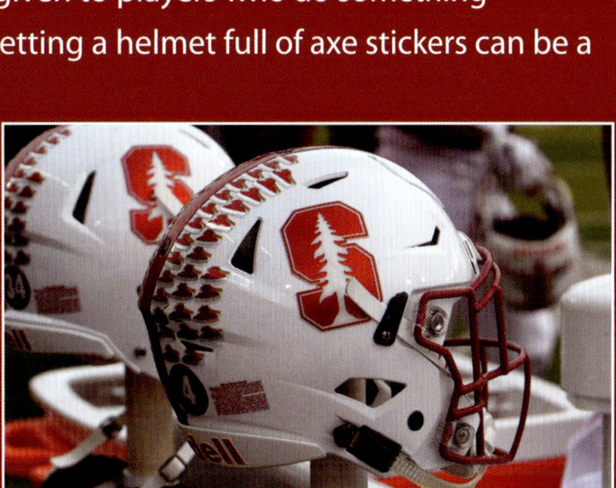

Stanford's axe helmet stickers are based on the Stanford Axe trophy, which is awarded to the winner of the yearly game between the Cardinal and the University of California Golden Bears.

Student Athletes

Only about **1 out of 50** college football players go on to play professionally.

Wide receiver Osiris St. Brown, who is fluent in three languages, was recruited by Notre Dame but chose to play at Stanford for academic reasons. St. Brown averaged 25.1 yards per reception during the 2018 season.

Being a college student athlete is hard work. Student athletes have to perform well on the football field and in the classroom. Stanford student athletes are required to meet a minimum grade point average and attend all of their classes. They must also have 12 academic credits per term. Stanford student athletes have access to the Athletic Academic Resource Center, where Stanford offers many services to help them balance the student athlete life.

Many student athletes are given athletic scholarships. An athletic scholarship is a financial aid agreement between the athlete and the college or university. Athletes who do not receive an athletic scholarship can be "walk-on" members of the team. This means they are on the team, but without athletic financial aid. Stanford typically awards the maximum number of football scholarships allowed, which is 85.

Stanford linebacker Gabe Reid credits a long line of football-playing relatives for his pass-rushing skills and intensity on the field. Reid's father and uncle played in the NFL, and several other family members played football in college.

Bowl Games

Bowl games are held in **16** different states and **two** different countries, the United States and the Bahamas.

Stanford defeated the University of Wisconsin 20–14 in the 2013 Rose Bowl, making head coach David Shaw the first African American coach to win a Rose Bowl.

Bowl games are a unique sports tradition in college football. In the beginning of college football, there was no true **postseason**. Today, a variety of postseason bowl games are played. Bowl games give teams the opportunity to continue striving for recognition and victory after the end of regular play. There are currently 40 bowl games played in various combinations each year. These games are chosen with input from teams, sponsors, and the College Football Playoff Selection Committee. The game matchups are announced in December.

The Cardinal have played in many amazing bowl games. Their first appearance was in the 1902 Rose Bowl. The Rose Bowl is one of the oldest bowl games in college football. Stanford has won that game eight times. It has also won seven other bowl games, and has made it to a bowl game every year since 2009.

Texas Christian University (TCU) has a 3–0 win record in games against Stanford. The TCU Horned Frogs narrowly defeated the Cardinal in the 2017 Alamo Bowl with a score of 39–37.

The Coaches

Pop Warner is credited with inventing **shoulder and thigh pads**, saving players from painful injuries.

Stanford head coach David Shaw played football for the Cardinal from 1991 to 1994. Shaw coached in the NFL for 10 years before returning to Stanford Stadium as one of Jim Harbaugh's assistant coaches, and was promoted to head coach when Harbaugh left the team for the NFL.

The head coach is an important person who guides a football team through its practices and games. In Stanford history, there have been 34 different coaches leading the team. Of those 34, 11 coaches took the team to bowl games, and 8 claimed conference championship wins. With all the success past coaches have had, the head coaching job at Stanford is one of the most prestigious in the NCAA.

POP WARNER Glenn Scobey "Pop" Warner may be best known for the national youth football organization that shares his name. He is also known as one of the best coaches in college football history. From 1924 to 1932, he led the Cardinal to 71 wins. Warner is regarded by many as one of the best football coaches ever.

JIM HARBAUGH When his father coached at Stanford in the 1980s, Jim Harbaugh went to high school across the street from Stanford Stadium. Cardinal football was a big part of his past when he took over as coach in 2007. In 2009, Harbaugh led Stanford to the Sun Bowl, which was its first bowl appearance since 2001. He left Stanford in 2011 to coach the NFL's San Francisco 49ers, and later returned to college coaching at the University of Michigan.

DAVID SHAW The current coach of the Cardinal, David Shaw, has more wins than any other Stanford football coach. In his time leading the team, it has not gone a year without making it to a bowl game. Shaw has never had a losing season and is regarded as one of the best college football coaches in the nation.

The Mascot

Although the Tree often appears on various "worst school mascots" lists, it is one of the most unique mascots in the NCAA.

While Stanford does not have an official on-field mascot, the Stanford marching band does. The Stanford Tree is one of the most iconic mascots in all of college football. Wherever the band plays, the Tree is there, dancing to the music and leading the fans in cheers.

The Tree first appeared in 1975, three years after the university decided to replace its old mascot, which was a Native American. It represents the redwood tree, which is the logo of the nearby city of Palo Alto. The Tree has been a fixture at games ever since. Unlike most team mascots, the Tree is **redesigned** every year. The student who dresses as the Tree gets to create the new mascot costume, a tradition unique to Stanford.

Students who want to become the next Tree participate in "Tree Week," an event judged by the current Tree, past Trees, and the Stanford Band. Hopeful Trees design a costume and perform skits and stunts to convince judges that they should become the next Tree.

Legends of the Past

For many players, their time with the Cardinal is the start of a promising football career. These are some of the best-known football players to play for Stanford.

John Elway

Known by many as one of the greatest quarterbacks of all time, John Elway is a Stanford **legend**. He came to Stanford in 1979 to play football and baseball, but football was where he really stood out. During his senior season, Elway led the nation with 24 touchdown passes. He was inducted to the College Football **Hall of Fame** in 2000. Elway played his entire NFL career with the Denver Broncos, until his retirement in 1998. In 2004, he was inducted into the Pro Football Hall of Fame.

Position: Quarterback
Seasons: 1979–1982 (Stanford Cardinal), 1983–1998 (Denver Broncos)
Born: June 28, 1960, Port Angeles, Washington

Christian McCaffrey

Christian McCaffrey was one of the most electric players in college football during his three years at Stanford. In his sophomore season in 2015, McCaffrey broke the NCAA record for all-purpose yards, finishing with 3,864. He was also the first Stanford player to rush for 2,000 yards in a single season. In his junior year, McCaffrey set the team's single-game rushing record, with 284 yards. After completing his junior year in 2016, he went to the NFL **draft** and was selected eighth overall by the Carolina Panthers, where he remains a vital part of their offense.

Position: Running Back
Seasons: 2014–2016 (Stanford Cardinal), 2017–Present (Carolina Panthers)
Born: June 7, 1996, Castle Rock, Colorado

John Lynch

John Lynch began his career as a backup quarterback. Before his junior season, his coach convinced him to make the move to safety, where he would eventually make his mark as a star player. After a season in which he had four interceptions and one defensive touchdown, Lynch decided to enter the 1993 NFL draft. He was drafted by the Tampa Bay Buccaneers in the third round and ended up playing 15 seasons in the NFL. Lynch transferred to the Denver Broncos in 2003, where he played until his retirement in 2007.

Position: Safety
Seasons: 1989–1992 (Stanford Cardinal), 1993–2003 (Tampa Bay Buccaneers), 2004–2007 (Denver Broncos)
Born: September 25, 1971, Hinsdale, Illinois

Richard Sherman

Before Richard Sherman became one of the most feared defensive backs in the NFL, he played wide receiver for Stanford. During his freshman year in 2006, he led the Cardinal in receiving yards, but after an injury, he asked to switch to cornerback. In this position, Sherman helped the 2010 team win a school-record 12 games. After graduating from Stanford, Sherman was selected by the Seattle Seahawks in the fifth round of the 2011 NFL draft. He won a Super Bowl with the Seahawks and has been named to four **Pro Bowls**. Sherman also led the NFL in interceptions in 2013. He now plays for the San Francisco 49ers.

Position: Cornerback
Seasons: 2006–2010 (Stanford Cardinal), 2011–2017 (Seattle Seahawks), 2018–Present (San Francisco 49ers)
Born: March 30, 1988, Compton, California

All-Time Records

10,911

Career Passing Yards

Steve Stenstrom holds the Stanford all-time passing yards record, with 10,911.

301

Rushing Yards in a Game

Bryce Love set a Stanford record when he rushed for 301 yards in a 2017 game against the Arizona State University Sun Devils.

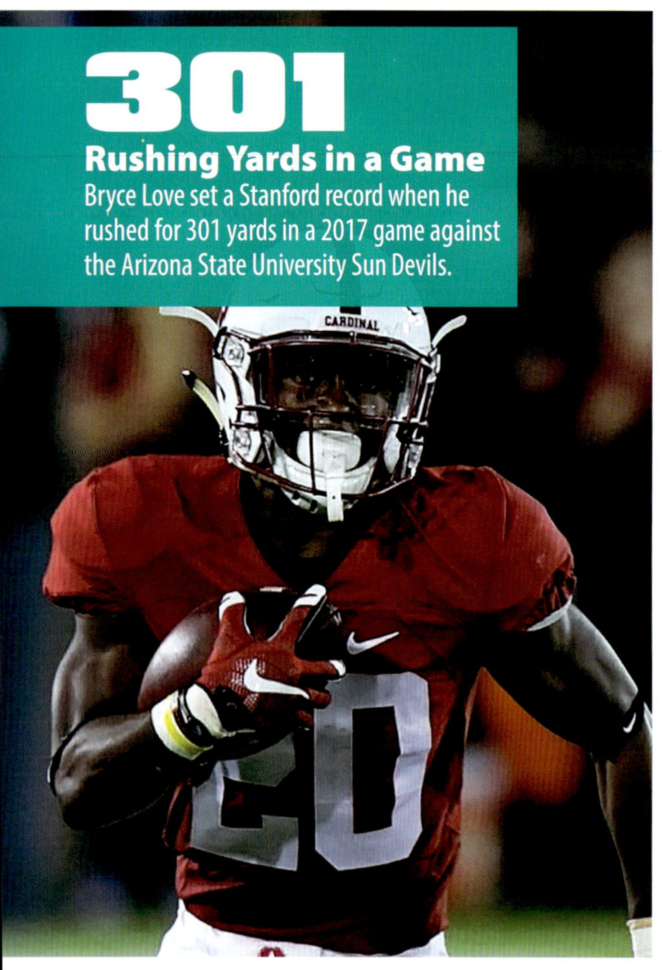

4

Single-Game Interceptions

In 1934 against the University of Washington Huskies, Bobby Grayson intercepted four passes, a single-game Stanford record.

37

Touchdown Passes in a Single Season

Andrew Luck threw for 37 touchdown passes in a season, the most in a single year for Stanford.

4,047

Most Career Receiving Yards

Troy Walters holds Stanford's records for the most single game, single season, and career receiving yards. From 1996 to 1999, Walters logged 4,047 receiving yards.

Timeline

Throughout the team's history, the Stanford Cardinal have had many memorable events that have become defining moments for the team and its fans.

1891
The first Stanford football team is formed.

1924
The team wins the Pacific Coast Conference title, its first conference championship.

1928
The team wins its first bowl game, defeating the University of Pittsburgh Panthers 7–6 in the Rose Bowl.

1900 1920 1940 1960

1926
Stanford finishes the season 10–0–1, its first undefeated season under Coach Pop Warner.

In 1958, Stanford scores its fewest points in a regular season, with only 93.

1970
Stanford wins its first Pacific-8 Conference title.

1979
John Elway begins his career as quarterback at Stanford.

The Future
After reaching a bowl game every year since 2009, the Stanford football team is primed to continue its success far into the future. The Pac-12 competition is tough, but under the leadership of Coach David Shaw, the future looks bright. Stanford is definitely a force for rivals to reckon with.

2015
Christian McCaffrey sets the NCAA record for all-purpose yards in one season.

2011
The Cardinal score a Stanford record of 561 points in a single season in 2011.

1980 2000 2020

1992
Cory Booker is named a Rhodes scholar, the only one in Stanford football history.

In 2012, Stanford wins its first Pac-12 conference title.

2018
The Cardinal win a tenth consecutive trip to a bowl game with a matchup against the University of Pittsburgh Panthers in the Sun Bowl.

Write a Biography

Life Story

A person's life story can be the subject of a book. This kind of book is called a biography. Biographies often describe the lives of people who have achieved great success. These people may be alive today, or they may have lived many years ago. Reading a biography can help you learn more about a great person.

Get the Facts

Use this book, and research in the library and on the internet, to find out more about your favorite player. Learn as much about him as you can. What position does he play? What are his statistics in important categories? Has he set any records? Also, be sure to write down key events in the person's life. What was his childhood like? What has he accomplished off the field? Is there anything else that makes this person special or unusual?

Use the Concept Web

A concept web is a useful research tool. Read the questions in the concept web on the following page. Answer the questions in your notebook. Your answers will help you write a biography.

Concept Web

Adulthood

- Where does this individual currently reside?
- Does he have a family?

Your Opinion

- What did you learn from the books you read in your research?
- Would you suggest these books to others?
- Was anything missing from these books?

Childhood

- Where and when was this person born?
- Describe his parents, siblings, and friends.
- Did he grow up in unusual circumstances?

Accomplishments off the Field

- What is this person's life's work?
- Has he received awards or recognition for accomplishments?
- How have this person's accomplishments served others?

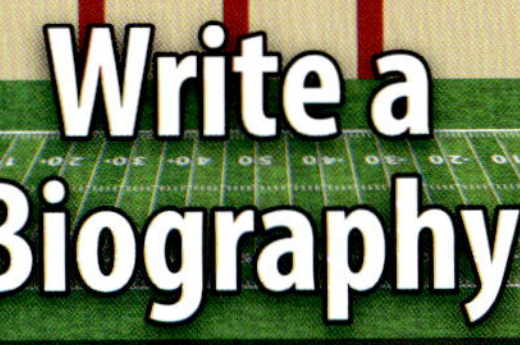

Help and Obstacles

- Did this individual have a positive attitude?
- Did he receive help from others?
- Did this person have a mentor?
- Did this person face any hardships?
- If so, how were the hardships overcome?

Accomplishments on the Field

- What records does this person hold?
- What key games and plays have defined his career?
- What are his stats in categories important to his position?

Work and Preparation

- What was this person's education?
- What was his work experience?
- How does this person work?
- What is the process he uses?

Trivia Time

Take this quiz to test your knowledge of the Stanford Cardinal. The answers are printed upside down under each question.

1 Which NFL team drafted John Elway?

A. The Denver Broncos

2 Who coached the Cardinal to their first undefeated season?

A. Pop Warner

3 What helmet stickers can players get for outstanding performances?

A. Stanford Axes

4 Who was the first Stanford player to rush for 2,000 yards in a single season?

A. Christian McCaffrey

5 Who is the current Stanford coach?

A. David Shaw

6 Who has been the only Rhodes scholar in Stanford football history?

A. Cory Booker

7 How many bowl games has Stanford won?

A. 15

8 In what year did Stanford football start?

A. 1891

9 What is the name of the Cardinal's home stadium?

A. Stanford Stadium

10 In what year did the Stanford Tree first appear?

A. 1975

Key Words

draft: an annual event where the NFL chooses college football players to be new team members

Hall of Fame: a group of persons judged to be outstanding in a particular sport

legend: an extremely well-known or famous person

logo: a symbol that stands for a team or organization

offensive: having to do with attacking the opposite team in order to score points

postseason: a sporting event that takes place after the end of the regular season

Pro Bowls: the annual all-star games for NFL players pitting the best players in the National Football Conference against the best players in the American Football Conference

redesigned: designed something in a different way than originally built or made

renovations: construction that works to improve or expand an older building

World Cup: an international soccer competition that is hosted by the Fédération International de Football Association (FIFA)

Index

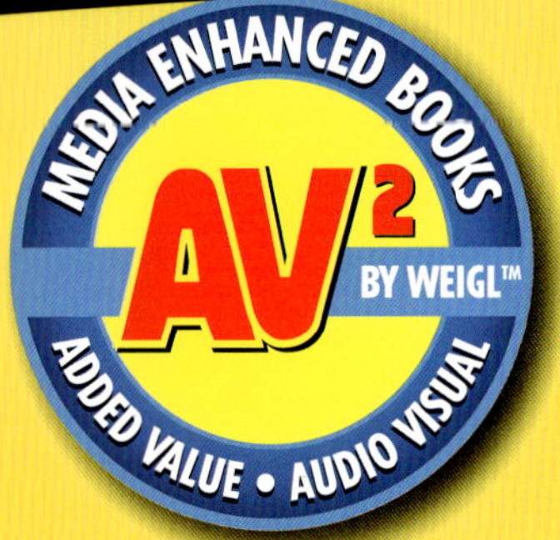

Log on to www.av2books.com

AV² by Weigl brings you media enhanced books that support active learning. Go to www.av2books.com, and enter the special code found on page 2 of this book. You will gain access to enriched and enhanced content that supplements and complements this book. Content includes video, audio, weblinks, quizzes, a slideshow, and activities.

AV² Online Navigation

Audio
Listen to sections of the book read aloud.

Book Pages
AV² pages directly correspond to pages in the book.

Video
Watch informative video clips.

Embedded Weblinks
Gain additional information for research.

Key Words
Study vocabulary, and complete a matching word activity.

Try This!
Complete activities and hands-on experiments.

Quizzes
Test your knowledge.

Slideshow
View images and captions, and prepare a presentation.

AV² was built to bridge the gap between print and digital. We encourage you to tell us what you like and what you want to see in the future.

Sign up to be an AV² Ambassador at www.av2books.com/ambassador.

Due to the dynamic nature of the internet, some of the URLs and activities provided as part of AV² by Weigl may have changed or ceased to exist. AV² by Weigl accepts no responsibility for any such changes. All media enhanced books are regularly monitored to update addresses and sites in a timely manner. Contact AV² by Weigl at 1-866-649-3445 or av2books@weigl.com with any questions, comments, or feedback.